PEBBLES ON THE SHORE – A COLLECTION

Other Books by Don Davison

An Outline of a Philosophy of the Consciousness of Truth
The Concept of Personhood in the Evolutionary Process of Being
The Game of Life: A Player's Manual for Executives and Others
Sign Posts: A Collection of Essays, Volumes I, II, III, and IV

Poetry

Thoughts and Feelings Book I
Thoughts and Feelings Book II
Needles from the Ponderosas at Zirahuen
Seeds from the Ponderosas at Zirahuen
Pitch from the Ponderosas at Zirahuen
Humus from the Ponderosas at Zirahuen
Sawdust from the Ponderosas at Zirahuen
Sun's Rays Bouncing off the Ponderosas at Zirahuen
Shadows Beneath the Ponderosas at Zirahuen
Cones from the Ponderosas at Zirahuen
Pollen Sifting from the Ponderosas at Zirahuen
Reflections from Lucerne
Searching Swamps
Questions
Time's Echoes
Memories
Insistences
Splashes
Ripples
Pebbles on the Shore

Collections

Always Extolling
Murmurings
Iris and Other Things
Pieces of the Journey
Through the Swamps of Time
Reflections from Lucerne
The Twelfth Hour

PEBBLES ON THE SHORE – A COLLECTION

Don Davison

Zirahuen Publishers
Tempe, Arizona

pathtotheself.com
DrDavison@pathtotheself.com

© Zirahuen 2013
All rights reserved. Published 2013
Printed in the United States of America

ISBN 978-0-9858130-2-4

No part of this book may be used or reproduced in any manner whatsoever without written permission except in the case of brief quotations embodied in critical articles and review.

Cover photo by Don Davison
Author photo by Patricia Davison

A special thanks to Louella Holter and to Tina Rosio from W.

To Patricia, for everything.

All of Don Davison's books have water on their covers. Water is one of the most essential attributes of the planet Earth; without it, life as we know it would not exist. It deserves our most considered attention.

Davison's collections of poetry all end with "Finding Pieces." Many of you have asked, where did the rules for the Game of Life come from? They come from many places and different times. Good hunting!

CONTENTS

O Ignorance	1
A Visit with the Dancing Muse	2
Worry Not!	3
There Is Just Love	4
Beacon on a Hill	5
A Voice Crying in the Wind	7
Bernardo!	8
A Writer's Rumination	10
Image and Likeness	11
Beyond Facebook	12
Splash!	14
The Wheel of Fortune	15
I Ask Myself	16
Neighbors	17
Three Statements and Some Questions	19
Tender Is the Guard	20
Seashore	21
A Humanistic Manifesto	22
Gratitude	24
The Challenge	25
Grandchildren	26
We Live in a Time …	27
God's Hour	28
Your Lies Unveiled	29
Let Them Speak!	30
I Don't Know	31
Plastic Flowers	32
Dilemma	33
Desert Peace	34
A Collection of Pieces	35

A Comment	36
A Direction	37
Always	38
An Observation	39
Close Enough	40
A Purposeful Presence	41
A Question for Our Times	42
Another Time	43
Are We the Romans?	44
Choosing	45
Let Me Speak!	46
What? Pay Attention!	47
A Mess on the Veranda	48
Celestial Fire	49
Now?	50
Always Walking – Always Running	51
Dedicated Ignorance	52
Fear Not!	53
His Light	54
It Was …	55
My Credo	56
My Friend	57
Praying	58
Be Careful	59
Such Fools!	60
Who Will Say …?	61
Reminds	62
Blank Slate – Not!	63
Talisman	64
Voice of the Father	65
Utterances	66
Remember	67
Fact	68
Where to Stand?	69
Waves	70

To Sin	71
Thank You	72
Time	73
A Now	74
Chimes	75
We Have Become	76
Hold It!	77
Herky-Jerky	78
I Live	79
Embracing	80
Just Enough	81
Life's Sacred Aspect	82
Dying Nationalism	84
Stillness	85
The Path	86
Thanks But No Thanks	87
Ignorance – Again	88
The Wroughtist	89

O IGNORANCE

Ignorance! Ignorance!
O Ignorance!
You bloody dirty thing!
We do not know what we do not know,
yet when we come to know,
we must also know
there was a time
when we did not know.
What humbling magnificence!
What joy!
To know that we can come to know
– that there is yet something –
for us to know.

A VISIT WITH THE DANCING MUSE

Why when I think I'm ready
do you linger at the edge of my conscience,
sword drawn,
feinting battle from the shadows,
hinting of some ancient truth,
or some current cataclysmic portent?
Come out!
Engage my soul in mortal combat!
Swing that mighty steel blade!
Attack! Defend! Intone those sacred mantras!
Shout eternal truths at those who lie and rob,
those whose apparent purpose
is to feed to all such ill-disposed
gluttonous wallowings.
Step forward you blessed and cursed diamon.
Rise up from your crouching-ready pose!
Move from shadow to the light
so that I may see your true intent
– and forewarn those fated brethren
who mock the justice of our age,
those who have forgotten
the purpose of their souls.

WORRY NOT!

Worry not!
Nothing that we say or do,
as of the now,
diminishes in any way the stillness
of wilderness moments
scattered across the enclaves
of nature's hidden swales.
Their serenity reigns supreme.
Meanwhile,
in our new-now,
the one we may choose for decision making,
we must take our cues from nature's
patterned efforts:
Not too fast.
Not too slow.
Never crowded, always enough,
within this margin of forever,
we are given to our choices.
So choose!

THERE IS JUST LOVE

"History does not run backwards,"
it has been written.
The decisions we make *now* matter
more than any piece of history.
This moment
– the one we are in right now –
this second
matters more than all the rest,
because of all the rest.
Do it now!
Do it now!
Do it now!
From *this still point*
we decide how we must face the next.

BEACON ON A HILL

Like a beacon on a hill
through the mists and fogs of time,
we stand in duty to our brethren.
Lead on!
We mumble in our tattered ill-fitting clothes
and with wizened voices utter prayers
to those who've gone before.
We hear whining, whimpering, sniveling,
dribbling from untutored lips.
Yet we,
like Prometheus,
must shoulder the burdens of the ages
and mount again our hill.
We must see the light
so long denied our festering souls.
Shine on O Light of our redemption!
Lead us towards freedom's gate
where stands the narrow pillars,
guards of life's salvation.
Beckon us on O Light
of chaste and holy purpose!
Guide us through night's perils
where lost from you we screamed and cried,
shoved and pushed our neighbors
from our doors.
O Mother of our heathen souls
birth again resolves.
Embrace we must,
the democracy of hidden times
where blood was shed in sacrifice
to children yet unborn.

There must come a time
when turning towards the bright and hopeful eyes
of children,
we grip again the tiller of our ship.
Lead on O Light!
Feed the hungry souls lost from sight.
Lead on to greater understanding of our purpose!
To stand for one and one for all
in holy space
is gift enough in rift and race.
Draw us on through storms of ignorance
and petty pace.
Slumber not and tarry little,
we have eons yet to go.
Onward!
Onward towards the light
to an ever greater democratic right!
We owe this to all who've known the night.
Carry on through tempests of idle thrill
towards that beacon on the hill!

A VOICE CRYING IN THE WIND

Stand still! Feel! Sense!
Come to know your presence in the hub-bub,
the anxiety-ridden madness
and the magnificent tranquility of the present.
There are untold treasures in the boreal sweeps,
in the Amazon mists, in the desert sands,
on the Nordic shores.
The quiescence of eternity waits
in the shrouded time of our planet.
Be not deceived by the eclectic synaptic
dissonance of our current moment.
This too shall pass.
We will treat ourselves and our children
to the depths of solar silence
where shadows dance in graceful glee
and the music that we hear
is His, ours, everyone's.

BERNARDO!

Yes!
That's it!
Bernard, St. Bernard of Clairvaux.
When was the last time I read from his works?
Now there was an incredible loving soul!
So,
when was the last time you read
the life of a sacred wonderer?
If you say never
I will be tempted to place you
in that heap of humanity
that has chosen to become Machado's Don Nada,
Don Nadie, Don Nunca.
(Sir Nothing – Sir No One – Sir Never)
And when was the last time
you wrote a letter
to your mother, father, grandmother, grandfather,
and wept?
How long has it been?
If you say yesterday I will smile knowingly.
If you say last month
I will admonish you to partake of a penance
that will press home to you
that glorious truth –
Without them where would you be?
Such a little thing,
taking only minutes
assuages so much guilt.
Stand still in silence and weep!
They may too,
after receiving a missive long overdue.
Take the time to cry and write!
Yes, I know you can phone.

It isn't the same.
A wave of emotion may catch both of you
and yet the practiced tongue moves on.
Write!
Ride those waves,
those crests and troughs!
Languish in the depths of remembrances!
Hold those human moments!
Seek reverence!
Remember those Irish monks
isolated from the chaos of the world
laboring in sequestered space
saving knowledge for souls' banquets.
What vision of the greater good
drove them to their daily tasks?
Where is that image from,
and of what, in such a holy place?
A focus is a must.
Amid mental machinations and a pounding heart
the rhythm of the eternal now
is so difficult to grasp.
Breathe in serenity!
The trees do not scream in impatience.

Know your purpose!
Work well done today
prepares one for the morrow.
Full of ideas and in haste,
I enter my office.
Looking and looking for a pencil,
I finally find one.
Needing a better point,
I turn and find a waiting arsenal
next to my sharpener.
When was the last time I came to my cell?

A WRITER'S RUMINATION

When crashing pixilated abstractions,
accompanied by bombastic explosions,
assault eyes and ears,
we turn to words.
Minds struggle in transition.
In some heroic attempt at understanding,
we swim in vast seas of pollinated forms
reminding us of the overlays of reality.
Spiked balls of touching tentacles
stretching into space,
much like information bits,
are cast amongst our fathomings.
An "I" lingers,
isolated from the center
of a liquid flowing of mechanics
that spreads the process of life maintenance.
We call them intergalactic interactions
of bio and astrophysics.
While in rampant succession
rural and urban nuclei burst
in powerful expressions,
casting seeds
to raging winds and torrents,
creating new life forms needing love.
And all this lies
in the firmament of words.

IMAGE AND LIKENESS

I am an I am!
Pulled into being by my real selfish-self,
exuding an integrity of being,
saying "Yes!" to all I am,
becoming all that I can be,
all that I must be,
all that I am –
a gift of the Giver,
giving my me to my loving-self,
to all others and to my God.
I am an I am!

BEYOND FACEBOOK

People gape in awe at the Sudan's
"splitting independence"
and the "Egyptian moment of freedom."
They wobble on one leg
without a good prosthetic,
failing to realize the need
of an interim pair of good crutches
before they learn to walk again –
that those essential tools
of faith and courage
allow us
– again –
to set our souls free.
In the aftermath of the ripples
of the arch liberal's insipid adolescence
and the arch conservative's staid stupor,*
the main body of humanity
continues to surge forward,
knowing full-well that
"history does not run backward."**
There has always been that critical mass
of sufficient focus,
articulated so well by our enlightened
Greek brethren,
"stay the middle course –
not too much of this
and not too much of that."

In the depths of our bowels
and the heights of our hearts
humanity knows we always need three,
me, you,
and the awe-inspiring "Other"
leading us to ourselves.
Beyond Faceook,
we need to learn to see the reflection of the eternal.

* See "Embracing," on page 80.
** "History Does Not Run Backward" is in *The Twelfth Hour: A Collection.*

SPLASH!

In the waters of the mind,
we find it all.
Every finely tuned speck of dust,
some light, some heavy,
bears witness.
In the furnace of consciousness,
we forge the metals of a person's dreams:
Freedom! Freedom!
Always freedom to express
what is eternally already there.
And upon which the annealing of an age
must be met with courage.
A focused courage that sees the light,
and not being blinded
– because it is as yet not too close –
can see the path.
In that synergism that flutters
like shadows of fall,
we courageously seek the Holy Grail
of self as a Divine expression.
A voice sings, "Alleluia, amen! Amen alleluia!"
And in that euphoric moment
comes the question,
Whose soul are we saving?
And from the silence the answer,
The All's, mine, everyone's.

THE WHEEL OF FORTUNE

Before us stands the wheel of fortune,
the wheel of fire.
Consciously fear presents itself,
even though it does not come first.
Love – union,
belonging comes first.
A knowing of togetherness
that gathers from the eternal void
what one needs, or wants.
It all comes from the tips of fingers,
from the surface of every cell,
the tongues of being.
The whole is our goal.
We extend. We feel. We touch.
Matter becomes mind!
The Man of the Mancha says
"Come! Enter into my imagination
and see him as he really is."
With that line we begin our journey,
"*The Impossible Dream*"
is the dream we all must dream
– if we are human.

I ASK MYSELF

I ask myself –
where does order lie,
in the random beating heart of the universe,
or in the freedom of present's choice?
From the eclectic farness of relativity
and the infinitesimal closeness of the quantum
comes space/time.
So …
standing in the present-midst of babbling ideologues,
can we still see in the cock of a child's head,
and in the intentful gaze of a child's eyes,
the eternal expression of a within reaching out,
a sentient soul's center
touching another?

NEIGHBORS

Two neighbors caught in time's web –
one mixed and confounded
in a history of conquest and a "labyrinth of solitude,"
then pushed into our now –
the other on freedom's bent,
in the arrogance and exuberance of youth
with much to do,
moving too far too fast
and missing the seasonings of age.
Then,
they too were thrust upon the stage.
Neither can have a respect for truth and laws
without an ownership of maturity that says,
"Now is our time to forgive and to give,
me – you, you – me,
and upon a new pedestal of wisdom,
birthed in the implosion of a new time,
they can choose again the rights of truths:
"We are all one."
And to those who divine formulas
that they, themselves,
fathom only in a fog and then say,
"Well, maybe …,"
none of you are exonerated from your guilt.
If you lie and steal, you lose!

We have all been liars and thieves.
Immigration's rules are always what we make of them,
and in the end,
in a new space/time,
evaluated with the magnanimity of reflection
on a right and a wrong.

We can then forgive ourselves and others
while we choose to create a brighter history.
This will be a history of new laws,
laws reflecting new guiding principles:
we will identify ourselves,
and we expect you to do the same.
Neighbors must know one another well.
We must,
with a reasoned magnanimity
devoted to responsibility,
reach across the boundaries of space
and cultural pace.
There is no other way.

THREE STATEMENTS
AND
SOME QUESTIONS

We all start from some place –
with what is already there.
The difference of an age and age
is growing up.
We move from pieces to a broken piece.
Are we ever of one peace?
Why is it that on the threshold of consequences
we find blame?
Why is it that tunnels intrigue us
– just a bit?
Where is the maiden who becomes the Lady
and where the youth who becomes the Knight?
To slay the beast is one thing;
to sacrifice the beast
is quite another.

TENDER IS THE GUARD

Tender is the guard
who wrestles from the wind
the mistlettes of the storm.
What great purpose awaits
the captured essence of the sea?

SEASHORE

When will we open our minds and hearts
to the real beauty of the seashore,
with its ever-changing magnificence,
those oohs and aahs,
instilling a false connection of tranquility?
Each wave comes wearing, tearing, and building.
Would it be that we could see in each wave
the movements of humanity
and come to know
that to each time and to each shore
there is a glory all its own?
How wonder-full it would be
for each person
to take the stand-points of their time
and mine
from their depths,
gifts full of reciprocities,
giving to each,
and recognizing from each,
their all?

A HUMANISTIC MANIFESTO

If it is as it has been said –
"We are the rational social animal,
a homofaber, a destroyer,
a symbolizing, freedom loving,
soul seeking, sentient being" –
then this is what we must be about.
Our being mandates
a religiously societal response to life.
Therefore:
In the face of the all,
petty and great wars of history,
natural disasters and economic upheavals,
humankind has risen to the tasks
of forming and reshaping
the personhood of the species.
Always pushing, always pulling
ourselves and others
above the mundane drudgery
towards the ecstasies of life's challenges.
And now it is,
at this very moment,
when idealism and madness
seek to slaughter and to stalemate
the human effort,
when the implosion of the species accelerates
as technology makes possible the sharing
of vast amounts of information
to destroy, or to save,
that we must accept the challenges
of our current moment.

There is only this now upon which to build
with a manifest spirituality
based upon an understanding of the organic
and the astrophysics of the day.
And so...
with the accumulated spirit of the species,
we must again set sail
on this ocean of humanity.
This is the great work of the present,
the destiny
of the combined efforts of the ages.
Let us dedicate ourselves
to the saving of our kind,
and as Teilhard de Chardin said,
"As the earth gets a new skin,
or better still finds its soul,"
we will be able then to sift and winnow
truths scattered throughout
the body of our humanity.
From accolades to conquerors
we must move on to new roles,
roles that teach us how to save
and how to protect.
To the scientists, technicians,
saints and sages, to all of the age:
May we seek to touch the holy
in order to save ourselves
and rededicate our focus
to the saving of us from ourselves.

GRATITUDE

To know that in this life
I was blessed with the opportunity
of coming upon an alpine meadow in late fall
and to envision the building of a cabin
to protect the members of a family
from the marauding winds
of the seasons and of time,
to create an expression of soul,
and to share the warmth
and inspiration of a hearth
with my wife, my children, and friends,
I am eternally grateful.

THE CHALLENGE

The purpose of space/time
is to strengthen,
in its own time and place,
the products of the ages.
Our challenge,
in sorting things out,
our selves included,
is to wait upon the truth
while
searching for the truth.

GRANDCHILDREN

Come, you vessel of great purpose,
you creature of light!
Oh, grandchild of mine,
to you I bequeath the future
of smoke and mirrors,
pain and pleasure.
Did I stroke your hair enough,
share enough my presence?
Will you,
when the foibles and fancies
begin their seductions,
stand against them with an iron will?
Will my prayers echo in your soul
as you race, crawl, struggle and fall,
will you rise again and shout
"Woe to the wicked!"
and then with staunch unbowed determination
continue your walk with a brave heart
up history's hill?*

*You may wish to see "History's Hill" in *Murmurings: A Collection.*

WE LIVE IN A TIME ...

We live in a time
when the what of the now
entered the who of the now
and snapped a piece off.
While fragments of the self
floated in a turbulent sea,
attachments
to the wandering with-outs of others
were only subjects of our wonder.
We remained caught,
lost by the seaside eddies,
asking ourselves,
What should be done to save us
from our frenzied apathy,
as we choose to watch another episode
of Survivor, of 24?

GOD'S HOUR

God's hour is always ours.
He said it was so.
It must be so.
Yet we hurry,
stumbling along His paths,
claiming to be
"the thinker."
In our hubris we shout,
"We are the knowers!"
Meanwhile,
we forget the slug moving toward
its consummation,
and the bonding and rending of the elements.
Their purpose is theirs, ours is ours.
Be vigilant!
is the mandate of the Divine.
I take this to mean –
own the purpose that
the "I am" has set for you:
Love one another!
Hold another's hand.
And that is all.
Until –
the eternal *Then what?*
presents itself.

YOUR LIES UNVEILED

You lie!
You murdering bastards.
You give money to someone else
to do your killings.
You say you believe it is wrong
to kill your own.
I say unto you –
Allah, blessed be His Name,
knows the difference.
You hide in a child's fear –
an old testament fear.
You lose!
you ignorant, lily-livered
bastards of humanity.
You are the craven underbellies of the species.
Be damned!
There will be those "others"
who will take the fire, the sword,
and confront your ignorance
for themselves and for your own,
the ones you so defile.
May Allah be praised.

LET THEM SPEAK!

To the twisters and spinners
of the events and deeds of humankind's
illustrious and pathetic story,
I say this:
Don't touch history,
you destructive bastards!
History belongs to itself.
It stands as Janus stands with two faces.
One looking ahead and one behind,
the good and the bad,
the tragic and comic.
We are inclined to ask,
"Which mirrors the truth of our perception?"
They both speak.
Let them speak!

I DON'T KNOW

Amidst the terror,
the starvation,
the mutilation,
the pontifications,
the stupidities,
the futile attempts,
"What do we do when the children come?"
Stop the insanities!
Love them!

PLASTIC FLOWERS

I judged too quickly
from the appearance of an age.
The first tries were gaudy.
I forgot –
all things move,
and they move according to their own kind,
in their own time.
Now you can hardly tell the difference
in sight and touch.
Ah!
But where, oh where in Battle Star Galactica
will holograms be tucked away?
You can't hold them.
You can't smell them.
We are the sentient ones,
and if not,
we aren't.

DILEMMA

What says the logic of a soul
watching another soul destroy itself,
and others?

*

The choices are:
Walk away.
Kill the soul to save it from itself
and to protect others.
Hold the soul until it feels connected
to the purpose of love.

*

Hint –
God has already chosen,
the soul is here.

DESERT PEACE

While otherwise engaged
behind a bush,
next to a mostly deserted highway
in Texas,
I felt and heard the passing of intermittent
roaring 70 mph vehicles.
The interludes of peace,
between the dissonance,
were awesome.

A COLLECTION OF PIECES

Nothing is as dramatic as complete integrity.
It just needs a little push here and there,
and as well,
a hand everywhere.
In order for there to be understanding,
we must perceive through the context
of that which is understood.
The myths and legends of time
and the reality of the present
are our battle fields.
It is precisely because we know
enough of the good things
that we get angry at the bad things.

A COMMENT

There is the swaggered pace
of the idiots
and the cautioned pace of the hunter.
In the hunter, we see the application
of the prudence of understanding history.
The swagger denotes
no understanding of anything.
From where comes the nonsense
of being stupid?
Media's glorification
of subversive involvement
(read here action/adventure)
has given further impetus
(there will always be a few crazies)
to activity that is not in the best interests
of Humankind.
I use this word because
I like to think that continued use
(that which is seen more often seems to stick)
is helpful in the learning process.
By definition –
if we don't adapt *we die*!
Let's learn to be *kind* enough
to survive.

A DIRECTION

In the great reciprocity of being's
directionality of efforts,
there must be a right and a left hand.
This truism stands rewarded
in the laboratories of the ages.
We must also know
that in this there is intent.
There is in all the thrusts and drags,
a coming and a going,
into the arms of Serenity
and out of her arms.
There is that forever yesness
that murmurs and shouts,
"I am!"
an eternal repetition of the voice
of the burning bush.
As mirth again escapes pursed lips,
from that oft-maligned eternal well of hope
there gushes forth an understanding of the ages:
"A Presence!"

ALWAYS

As the pendulum swings,
so too does one foot step ahead of the other.
The rocking of the cradle
mirrors the ebb and flow of the tides.
The lunar months move from full
to crescent.
Never is there anywhere nothing.

AN OBSERVATION

There is a generic wholesomeness
to our humanity.
We are a loving kind.
Our challenge is to stay the course,
to follow our star.
It is forever shining its light
upon our path.
It has been said,
"Make straight the way!"
We are struggling in our attempts.
"Strengthen our resolve,"
must be our clarion.
See the truth of our human presence.
We are Your gifts of self to selves.

CLOSE ENOUGH!

It's all in the arc of the throw –
the trick is
to let go in time.
Then it is,
that we come to know
close enough!

A PURPOSEFUL PRESENCE

Emanating
from all the great Coliseums of our day,
we feel the spirit of a presence
and focused intent,
manifesting in millions and millions
of spectators and athletes,
all participating in exercises
of effort and of hope.

A QUESTION FOR OUR TIMES

Will the young mixed-puppies of a culture
be seduced by the old corrupt behemoths?
The electoral jury is hung at 49/51 –
and tipping to the more-than side
of enough – even too much.
So tell me,
when the youthful exuberance
for the fashionable
and the branded-moment wears off,
will we fall victims
to the corruption of soul
where the waves of avarice
roll across the mainland?
Will there finally be more than
a few who will say,
"Enough of your tasteless shoving
of corruption down the throats
of your own constituents
in your all-out attempt
to do it to everyone!
Have you finally
"torn off enough faces"?*

Fiasco: The Inside Story of a Wall Street Trader by Frank Partnoy.

ANOTHER TIME

Caught in a somber assessment
of my personal pedantic history and an age,
I slipped into a wonderment of the negative
of some of our species' activities.
Then I thought of the Pillars of Creation,
and laughed.

ARE WE THE ROMANS?

Fear has driven our loins
to a sickness beyond despair –
we are held standing
only by an arrogance of ignorance.
We will soon fall to our knees
in abject senseless whimpering.
Cries will come from throats
too sore to speak.
Left without words,
we will have no way
to guide ourselves,
we will sink to our bellies
and crawl into the shadows.
Our pseudo courage will evaporate,
we will be gone from the human stage.
There will remain only a few,
the stalwart dreamers of wisdom with soul,
those who will rise up
and walk towards the altars of truth.

CHOOSING

I can choose to stand naked in the wind
and say,
"Yes and no" to Satan.
Yes to an existence, no to its allure.
I can also say,
"Yes, yes, and yes again!"
to an existence, to self-ownership,
and yes to a complementing presence.

LET ME SPEAK!

At the dawn of our pursuit
comes the whisper of the logos,
"I am here!"
An emanation incorporating
I am! You are! And all that will be!
The most intimate of our companions,
stalwart giver of advice,
a mischievous wonderer.
How is it that we live from that
ephemeral mused mind,
so collaborative, so independent?
What straight line can we expect
from such spiraled intentions,
centered and arcing away
only to be pulled again towards the center?
We live haunted,
pursued by the whispering one,
now this way, now that,
to know or to perish in the rhythm
of our machinations.
We labor only with our intentions
fed by the passion of yes,
curbed by the doubt of no.
In the face of this already perfect
cacophonous companion's subtle suggestions,
mysterious messages,
I leave my markings to cause myself, and hopefully another
to stand and be recognized,
and not just by others, but by one's own
homing-self in the face of abandonments and howling crowds.
I seek to present opportunities to shift a gaze,
inspire a movement, hearken to a call,
illicit an obligation.

WHAT? PAY ATTENTION!

Time has given us the gifts of time:
Plant! Tend! Harvest!
Beware the bloating nothingnesses
as they flash incessantly away from the light.
We must cup the chalice of our mates in tender's time
and fondle tips to life's gentle purpose.
Be gone you savages of wanton ignorance!
Tread not where life is left and softness reigns.
Leave it alone!
Embrace it all!

A MESS ON THE VERANDA

Found –
lying in a crumpled mass,
silver tubes, cords,
(one broken like a wing hunting air)
and wood.
What notes could issue forth
evoking celebrations of life?
I tied a knot of severed ends.
Voila!
The audience,
a pair of geckos and me
with front row seats
and nature all around.
A roaring screaming jet's notes
crosses chimes scale.
And,
for a fleeting second,
the wind, the chimes, the ear, the plane,
and me are one.

CELESTIAL FIRE

I live in a cave of an ardent heart.
A bed of coals forms my resting place.
My imprisoned self cries out
from the center of the cosmic furnace,
seeking the soul of that cataclysmic beginning –
the birth of life itself.
A glowing warmth of present purpose
shrouds Divine's intentions,
separating and uniting in a cauldron
the celebration of sacred freedom.
May I learn to love myself
as His gift of me to me
as I share myself with the rest of His creation.

NOW?

Born into my time and out of my time,
how am I to find a new beginning?
Not in the eclectic morass
of the electronic archipelago,
much streaking at e-speed,
inaccessible to tired eyes and an old mind.
No!
It must be from simple form
(albeit from an inexhaustible fountain)
that catches space and holds
a self hung-up
on intimate presence.
In my before-time,
I remain welcoming
those apprehendable infinite progressions
of sacred stuff.

ALWAYS WALKING – ALWAYS RUNNING

Walking in the shadow,
running toward the Light,
life is the "I am!"
of existence over time.
The confirmation of presence –
the becoming of the beating heart of God,
the still-point in the thrownness –
the yesness of the breathing of it all.
Still,
seeking the heart,
we walk and run in the mind.
We see with such clarity
in the dark thought of night.
We are "the in between."
We shout, "Lech'hiem!"
Then we silently, prayerfully, breathe,
"Awesome!"
Time is spent
running and walking over the bridge
seeking to gather the other one in love,
the one of self,
the One of all.

DEDICATED IGNORANCE

The creeping tide of humanity surprises us
and frightens us.
Presenting choices to enmesh ourselves
in the onslaught,
to have the feckless hope
of a romantic choice, or
to live on the edge –
trying to stay slightly ahead of the wave.
We try and try and try to fight
the inexorable,
changes, flows, flashes, crashes,
opportunities.
The question:
How to succeed when we inherited
a dedicated ignorance?

FEAR NOT!

Little did the Hellhounds conjure
the intrepid soul of person.
Their cries and howlings,
their paw scrapings sifting into the twilight,
did nothing to discourage the journey of our kind.
Whether in births or deaths
the soul sets sail on an infinite sea
girded by the deepest gift of knowledge:
"We are!"

HIS LIGHT

We carry the diamond of history
on our backs.
We cannot escape its shackles.
The facets of "mine" and "yours"
always catching different light.
Who is to say,
when all is said and done,
who was right?
It's all His light.

IT WAS ...

There was hard upon me
the winds of my time.
I laid away moments of reflection
and it came to me to write of them.
Across *Those Far Horizons** of the ages
sentiments wandered in
and about my presence.
Head-winds of druthers,
tail-winds of life,
all mingled with my present purpose.
And the moving hand wrote
of blessings and of curses.
All left tracks upon the land.
Yet,
there was always a
to do
that sat upon the threshold of my days.
To forge ahead and greet
the swells of tomorrow
or to lie in history's wake –
is the choice of freedom's thrust.

---

* "Those Far Horizons" is found in *Iris and Other Things: A Collection.*

MY CREDO

I say again and again,
"organic spiritualism" is the all of alls.
And don't be so naïve as to assume
this is some kind of pantheism.
In this vast mosaic of ecstasies and sorrows,
I take my inspirations
and wallow in my conundrums.
I wander and I await that next gentle breeze,
that shaft of golden light,
a lonesome loon call,
the gray pink of the early morning awakening,
that subtle quiescence of the vespering sunset
– and your gentle presence,
a touch that sends shivers
through every cell in my body
and every synapse of my brain,
that shuddering of soul that sets me free.

MY FRIEND

Tall, tall among men,
he shared a vibrant presence
that shattered silence and spoke volumes,
his eclectic artistic visions boiled
from Nature's Cauldron.
Starting in the middle of any log,
they went to the top
and to the bottom of every tree.
It was then,
in a sweeping vision of all his surrounds,
that a glorious imagination took flight.
Entering realms
of the eternal and infinitesimal,
he bathed his mind, heart, and soul
in the organic.
Whether sculpting or carving,
he was uncovering delicious delights
wrought from a palette he shared
with the Creator of all things.
And I, such a lowly man,
I was blessed to call him friend.
Still,
I see him now and then
striding along the banks of Thompson Creek,
standing in his prairie.
"As it was in the beginning, is now,
and ever shall be …"
Thank you for sharing your life with me.

For Bernard Roberts

PRAYING

I sit gazing through the boughs
of hemlock, cedar, pine, birch, willow,
and oak.
My Lucerne lies out before me.
Gentle ripples on the water
hint of time's passage.
I feel as though it is that I have arrived –
again.
Bathed in serenity my soul slips out
and soars through the North Woods.
I float across reflections in the lakes, streams,
and ponds.
I have come to breathe again in silent prayerful hope.
Thank you, Abba!

BE CAREFUL

Poetry is like petting a porcupine
– you don't do it very often.
And when you do,
you have to be very, very careful.

SUCH FOOLS!

And when did all this happen?
Well,
let me think …
I think it was sometime along
in the early years of the 21st century.
It was when most of the folks realized
that the media was overstocked with fools,
fools hell-bent on prognosticating nonsense
on just about every subject one could imagine.
Now,
while we are aware of the admonition
in the Good Book that no man should call
any brother a fool …
well, we just couldn't help it.
The facts were there,
we were here, and they were
spouting such incredible blather.
We just couldn't help ourselves.
"Them's fools for sure"
was the only thing we could agree upon.

WHO WILL SAY …?

As I wander in space and time
far from me
and far from mine,
I wonder,
Who will say Shabbat for me?
For now I am walking toward my grave
and from deep within a barrel chest I hear,
Adonai! Adonai!
Who will say Shabbat for me?
As ashes are passed from hand to earth
a tinkling of bells I hear,
Adonai! Adonai!
Who will say Kaddish for me?
Shufflings of thousands of feet
beat a cadenced chant and I hear,
Adonai! Adonai!
Who will say Kaddish for me?
The angels and their minions
raise their voices and I hear them,
Adonai! Adonai!
Such a wonder!
Who will say Shabbat for me?

REMINDS

A white silhouette catches my eyes.
Graceful steps encroach on feeding prey.
The hunting heron stalks the shore.
Reminds:
Pay attention or die!

BLANK SLATE – NOT!

We emerge once – and for the first time
as focused freedom
that already knows of the always.
God has written
with His stylus of forever
our name.
In acceptance of our gift of life,
we will in our own time
belong to Him.
It has been written.

TALISMAN

"What search ye, my son?"
"The Talisman of mine-for-ever."
They are always along our paths.
They present themselves as
a flash, a slight glint,
shimmerings on the shore
in time of draught or low tide,
the shallows through wet seasons.
We find them when in need of reflection.
Strolling the edges with our eyes on other times,
we encounter them along river banks, sea shores,
lakes, swamps, always sacred aspects of ourselves.
We stumble upon those sparklings of our saintly lore.
Stooping and reaching out we anxiously gather them.
Then turning them gently in our fondling fingers
great undulations of wonder swell souls
and our eyes dance in rainbow colors.
Startled and warmed hearts evoke.
Satisfaction flits across lips.
Hearts skip beats.
Furtive glances
take in our surrounds.
They are the alchemist's dream.
Lungs drink deeply in anticipation.
We move toward unfulfilled adventure.
New enjoyment emerges as a clear path.

VOICE OF THE FATHER

I invite you to come
– but you cannot stay.
Father I wander and I feel
the wonder that creates the eternal.
If so still
whence the effervescence?

UTTERANCES

"In Him, through Him, by Him."
I travel from my beginnings and my memories
to this opening,
this eternal window of His soul,
this forever-now of infinite yessness.
How can I compare my stations to His steps
from Pilot's palace to Golgotha?
I crawl and am ashamed to raise my head.
St. Bernard must have felt this way.
I am so, so sorry
for having touched pride's mantle
that never fit a human soul.
I have wrestled with the entanglements
of druthers when
there is only Your Way.
May I stay the course,
stray not from the path.
On knees with head bowed,
I can barely breathe out a heartfelt,
"Thank you."

REMEMBER

When wonder breaks upon a new shore
good things are bound to happen.
Grace grows
as truth meets the anvil of experience.

A FACT

Some poets write to an age,
others write to the ages.
How to do the latter,
which also does the former,
is my challenge.

WHERE TO STAND?

Caught on the wave of Manifest Destiny,
swept across a continent,
and sent around the world,
what we did
(for the most part)
was considered admirable.
Except for those times
when the baseness of the soul
captured battered hearts
and left us to our wanton selves.
We are as yet incomplete.
We must learn to
"stand still in silence"
to gain that essential self-perception
from which we direct the soul
to save us.
This will give
that stand-point of maturity that says,
"It all starts with me!"
We must govern for a one to a One
before we implode in our own naiveté.

WAVES

Rocking to and fro
– always held,
holding the "I am!"
of faith, hope, love.
Gifts of mirth
bestowing courage
– the heart-rage of love.
Left,
leaving
all to love
the All in the all.

TO SIN

The word has lost its meaning.
It's now all the name of cologne,
a deodorant,
merely a pastime for office fraternization.
And yet –
as our forebears scavenged carrion
from the edges of savannahs
in order to survive
so that we could be here now,
we disregard the purpose of our being.
We waste our time.
We dishonor their efforts
and the efforts of every fallen warrior.
As we seek more and ever more
venues of entertainment,
we sin against the efforts of humanity.
Rise up you fallen brethren!
Brave the day!

THANK YOU

When the early morning sunlight
lays its fingers on the needles
of the ponderosas
and paints with gold its first fall colors,
I greet the day and say
"Good Morning" to my God.
How brilliant are the gifts of dawn
that raise a heart to offer song.
And as my eyes return
from their window's journey,
I see my bedroom's nooks and crannies
touched by that same warm light.
It is then,
from the comforter's down-filled shield,
that I promise to make the most
of the gift of this new day.
To thee I give my thanks and trust,
from my weary body shake the rust.
Today I have so much to do,
first among them
thanking You.

TIME

Time sits heavy
on every person's shoulders.
Live free or die hard!

A NOW

Every person's presence
spans but a season in the great life of humanity.
Our challenge is to understand ourselves
in our own time.
How difficult it is to know
when life really begins
or when it ends.
As we were cast upon the shoals of our time,
we cast others upon the shoals of their time.
Not to batter them,
but in the sincere hope of offering them
a new freedom.

CHIMES

You are liken unto the Angelus Dei,
cymbals of the spheres,
harmonic resonances of
the All,
tinklings of the full chord,
pathways to eternity.
Calling out, beckoning,
startling the silence with your notes,
hinting of Heaven's Gate,
summoning to prayers,
thanks givings,
everyone an Alleluia,
infinite expressions of the Divine.

Found on a napkin among the scraps next to the political plates of those in Washington who attempt to devour each other in their current political arena.

An errant reflection capturing a truth by one of our elected officials ...

WE HAVE BECOME...

The mental largesse of the Post Modern world
shames the efforts of our ancestors.
Their attention to detail
and their studied commitment to common sense
gave a depth of focused effort
to their purpose.
And we,
we just wander aimlessly
and banter idiotically
in demonstrations
and court battles
wasting human effort.
From the courage and efforts of the species
we have become
pissants of anxious bacchanalia.

HOLD IT!

Ah, but how could a person not reflect
the scattered silver of an age
when one charges forward mimicking
the idiocies of an age?
The children who enter the forest –
these must return as adults
or they cannot bequeath
each their gifts of life.
We must be about the exercise of self-coincidence
as we travel the walkways of time.
When is it that we become soldiers
of the common good?
When is the mirror of our slumber
always broken by a new morning?
When we must rend the fabric of our culture,
even of our encumbered selves,
to bleed again the truths
of our own souls.

HERKY-JERKY

Too much we engage in spasmodic eclecticity
robbing us of that flowing of a known,
recognizable-one,
the one of our intentions,
the one following the dictates
of our wandering souls.
As the runner seeks a fluid stride,
faster, farther than the first
– in that same devout attention to purpose –
let us find the rhythm of our seeking-selves,
those blessed ends
that are our new beginnings.
Then solitude and acquiescence bathe us
in silent peaceful wonder,
still touching after shadows
left in warm dark soft folds of sheets
and airs of presence,
hinting history yet to come.

I LIVE

In the heat of August,
sweating in the cauldron of my mind.
Boiling information swirls in an accelerating vortex.
Dying images and words slip and crash
over a cognitive lattice
struggling to provide a perch,
a ledge, a crack,
in which to lodge.
Life slides over what is known,
crushing ephemeral synclines
of fleeting serenity.

EMBRACING

We came ill prepared to an age.
We have inherited a Dedicated Ignorance.*
Ensconced in pseudo-bucolic
sensitivities of mid-century frivolity,
unaware of the implosive dawning
of a new world,
we languished in a prolonged adolescence.
Numbers and technics mounted an old horse
garnished with the apocalyptic foreshadowing
of a devolution of ourselves.
Therein blossomed the idiocies of arch-liberal
and the intransigencies of staid-conservative.
These offer nothing
to enable a growing understanding
of communal opportunities,
nor for the exercising of responsibilities
in the sharing of our presence.
Embrace, we must,
the full spectrum of resources
and other life on the planet earth!
The time has come to plow the depths
of our very nature,
to emancipate the spirit,
and to act in love.
We need to rededicate ourselves to ourselves:
We are the loving species!

---

*See "Dedicated Ignorance," page 52.

JUST ENOUGH

From whence heroes,
those few who stand and see and do?
History's course crawls and races
over eons of our paths.
Always it has been a few
– *just enough* –
the righteous who have carried
burdens for the species,
protected the edicts and precepts,
the mandates and accords
that have birthed the laws
of humankind.
All lie sheltered in the shadows
of the great commandments,
those just laws that all have inklings for,
a few study,
and fewer still defend.
To those stalwart keepers of order for our kind,
those who do in spirit and in letter
the labor of the law,
lead on!
To live paying homage
to that spirit and those letters
for self and child is what makes us
worthy of those gifts of
just enough –
who knew enough to care enough,
who were responsible enough
and respected life enough
to protect life for freedom's sake.
May our prayer be
that enough will choose
to be one of those few.

LIFE'S SACRED ASPECT

In the face of death there is that orgasmic push,
a thrownness
that offers opportunities to wonder,
to grope, to need to touch, to hope,
to catch ourselves.
From blundering flashes to shadowed presences,
in synclines of stacked cells
hovering at the cliffs' edges of synapped space,
we gallantly hang on to our known-selves
refusing not to believe
that in the unknown effervescence,
we share in the Divinity's sacred mission:
Bringing more life to light.
All the while
hoping that enough sperm is cast and caught
that there will be one
to give birth to another who will know,
again,
the shadowed journey into self,
a self that always seeks another.
"Ella, ella una y quay …"*
She, she unites to crack the darkness with the light
so that we may see.
"Ello, ello una y quay …"
He, he unites to crack the darkness with the light
so that we may see.

I live to exercise the needing
of a seeking in the soul.
Knowledge is birthed from friction's heat
so that we may be consumed
in throes of life's intent.
What to call God –
when God is everything?
Tympanums!
I live to strike a hollow that gives a rhythm
to our soul's dance.
Empedocles,
you still stand thresholding the eternal twins
of love and strife.
May I know the one to embrace the other.

*See "Windspeak" in *Murmurings: A Collection*.

DYING NATIONALISM

The fated grotesque head
of the underbelly of humanity
turned its ugly face,
and in a final pathetic maligned gesture
a grimaced smile broke across
its scarred and torn countenance.
An almost inaudible
guttural wheezing gasp,
"I have slaughtered,
raped and maimed members
of every family of humankind
in the name of nationalism.
Finally,
I am becoming too old to matter.
But you,
you who have not taken enough time
and have not made the effort
to see and comprehend
the sacred oneness of the species,
to you I bequeath,
in the throes of my death,
sufficient leavings
hidden in my tattered cloak
for you to convince
the ignorant and the innocent
that there is still a fire
in the message of the differences
in the family called humankind.
Teach them to conspire
with the old lie
I used to bring millions to their deaths."

STILLNESS

From the rushing dissonance of the day
we must be still –
still enough to catch a glimpse
of the essence of stillness –
the calm repose in moss and fir.
We must come to know,
again and again,
the perfection of the moment.
By assuaging our fears
and embracing the holy quiescence –
then,
only then,
can we act in a sharing
of essential magnanimity,
setting to each
their freedom.

THE PATH

The modern person spends their time
compressing the horizontal,
both the lows and the highs of time.
What we spent too little time doing
was deepening the vertical,
plumbing the whys and wherefores
of the highs and the lows.
The understanding of life's
vagaries and joys
gives meaning to the journey,
puts the pieces together,
provides the woof and weave
of our purpose.
We have lost our way
in this postmodern moment.
We live in an aimless fixation
on the pieces.
We delight in the juxtaposition
and eclectic pace
when it is the whole that matters.
We have lost our sense of the sacred.
And worse,
we have lost our will to believe
that it is there.
We must rediscover the
Omnipresent
and place our trust in
Its path.
My prayer is that we find it again
for our sake and those of our children.

THANKS BUT NO THANKS

Audacity
will upon occasion
produce acceptable results,
and then a Custer's moment
proves the rule.
We have had
the audacity of hope.
It is nothing new.
What is new
is that synthesis of wisdom
that births a reasoned effort that says,
"Yes!"
to all those who hope
in some responsible way.
A way that gives to each an opportunity
to own their own responsibility
and provides that reasoned response
to personal and communal presence.
To this we say,
"Yes!"
In the soup of mutterings
we have heard smatterings of eloquence;
a PSA about being a father will do.
Yet,
when taken as a whole,
much is left wanting.

An excess of the exuberance of youth
doesn't get the job done.
It is time to say
"Thank you and good bye."

IGNORANCE – AGAIN

We are tumbled on a new shore.
In exhaustion, we crawl as children.
In exuberance, we prance as adolescents.
Raping the sensitivities of our elders,
we wreak havoc on our gifts.
We inherited a "Dedicated Ignorance"*
and a predilection for bad manners.
Our only portal providing any hope
to pay homage to our history,
ourselves, and the Giver,
is the gaining of sufficient experience,
presenting that supreme gift
of an informed choice,
a choice in which we exercise
a freedom complementing
what is eternally already here.

*See "Dedicated Ignorance," page 52.

THE WROUGHTIST

Prologue
(The Smithy)

We are all born of those early years
when awe births reflection
cementing our self to ourselves.
A young man stood and watched
the mighty arm swing the heavy hammer,
strike the glowing metal on the anvil.
For they are in you,
all those scenes from yesteryear
feeding the longings
of your soul.
The music of the blows bent time
to bonds of desires
knitting mind to heart.
Always fertile reflections
feed wonder's awesome pull.
Dreams were fed by memories
of the forge by day,
the hearth at night.
Bellows set the stage.
Tongs held each sacrifice.
The blocked piece
took the blows of the mind's intent.
To what purpose bent the back,
guided the movements of the hands?
Some things a young man's mind
wonders about.
Many things are understood only
after sufficient experience
seasons the heart and opens the soul.

> And yet,
> it is in the young that the die is cast.
> There are those antecedents
> that play surprising roles in the lives
> of humankind.
> The most significant
> always set a fixed course
> leading to those accomplishments
> that right the wrongs
> and bring a worthy sense of freedom
> to the expressions of fated purpose.

* * *

Such was the case with Will Wiley, a young man born into a time and a place that set the stage for one of those cross-over times, one that marked history with its abundance of thought, its creative genius, and those underlying human movements that change the very course of history.

The year 1650 was an exciting time in the city of Bristol. It was a bustling seaport with ships coming and going to all parts of the known world. Here, on the outskirts of the city, Simon Wiley chose to establish a small dairy, marry Elizabeth Wieker, and raise their family. The first child, a long-awaited son, they named William, after Simon's grandfather. They were later to have two daughters, Madeline and Alice. Maddy and Ali were omnipresent shadows following Will as they grew up and discovered their surrounding world.

And, as luck would have it, there was across the way a Blacksmith dhop. The smell of the forge and the banging of the Smithy's hammer reverberated from sun-up to sun-down. Will and his sisters imagined that their father and mother had made an arrangement with the Smithy to start the day by waking them from their sound sleep in the early mornings just in time for their breakfast and their chores. One might think that the children dreaded the clanging sound of the hammer on the metal and the anvil but that was not the case. In fact when they had a few moments to spare, Will and the girls would often cross the lane just to watch the wonders of the Smithy.

Will especially was enthralled with the whole process. He loved the whooshing sound as the bellows fed the forge and as the coals glowed and the stock changed color. He would watch the leathered hand grab with tongs the heated piece and lay it on the anvil and then the mighty arm of the Smithy would swing the hammer down with a loud Clang! then ting-ting, Clang! ting-ting. Will thought this sounded like a sort of music. During the conversations around the family table, he would extol the work of the Smithy, saying, "One day, that is what I will do."

Will's father had a penchant for reading and loved to talk to the neighbors about all sorts of topics and as well to all of the people who came to buy the milk, eggs, and cheese that the family produced and sold. He taught his children to read as the years went by. His mother, whom Simon had also taught to read, loved "the ideas of others" as she called the few books the family had and those that were lent to them by the local parish priest. Their main reading fare, however, consisted of the Bible, the new St. James Version, a gift from the bishop as a thank you for supporting the local parish. They would spend time every evening, just before the children were sent off to bed, reading and discussing the salient features of the Biblical narrative. The girls, when they were young, would start to nod and sometimes they would even fall asleep. Will, on the other hand, really enjoyed the stories and the explanations of what the parish priest called the "way of the book."

When Will was 12 he and his father often took a walk along the stream that crashed over the moss-laden rocks not too far from their home. It was late one Sunday afternoon, their day of rest, while discussing the many subjects of their lives, that Simon told Will that he was aging, and that he was looking forward to his son taking on more and more of the responsibility of the farm. Will listened carefully, but knowing what was in his father's heart, he hesitated to share his true feelings. Eventually they came to a log lying along the stream bank and laid out their "makings" for a small late lunch. His father watched his son's thoughtful gaze as it roamed over the surrounding countryside. "Will, what are thinking?"

Will turned to his father and said, "Father, you know I love what we do here with the farm and I understand that this is the way we make our living, but I have always dreamed of becoming a smithy. I love the smells of the forge and the wonderful things that can come from the anvil's surface. I love using the axe when I go out cutting the firewood. I love the hoe when I tend the garden, and also using the shovel when I clean out the barn. I would really like to be able to fabricate some of the beautiful fencing that surrounds the Cathedral and the graveyard in the city. There are just so many things that I would like to make of iron, things that last, things that can be used by others."

Will's father looked at his son and thought of his own life. His father had been a thatcher, and he had grown up helping to weave the heavy thick stalks into the protective roofing for the homes of the many families in the area. He remembered pausing in the laborious work as he, with the heavy bundles on his shoulder, ascended and descended the long ladder leading up to the roofs. He would pause and gaze across the meadows and fields at the grazing sheep and cattle. He loved the thick cream that they would pour on their porridge and wished with all his heart that he could have a never-ending source of that good tasting stuff.

He smiled at the remembrance of his youthful thinking, and reflected on the facts at hand: He had indeed "followed his own dream," and was glad of it. He thought about those simple ruminations of youth that rise up and motivate lasting desires to do what one really believes will lead to a busy, happy, productive life. They had actually led him to find a way to work on a farm and learn the art of animal husbandry and cheese making. All of which had indeed resulted in a wonderful family enterprise, one that provided excellent food for himself, his wonderful wife, and his beautiful children. He gazed at his young son and found himself sympathizing with his son's dreams. He thought to himself, "Well, when you come right down to it, I was the one who selected the parcel of land across the lane from the Smithy's shop."

"Well, son," he said, "I understand what you're feeling, and I respect your commitment to your dreams. I don't know how we'll run the farm without you but I will talk to George and see what he thinks about taking you on as an apprentice." Will's heart was filled with joy and he gratefully thanked his father for being his teacher and best friend.

That evening, as the family sat around the table, Simon said, "We will be having some changes around here in the near future. Will is going to start an apprenticeship with George and you girls are going to have to take on Will's chores." Will was overjoyed at the news and he looked over at his father and mother and could see how happy they were for their son. The girls were already busily dividing up his chores.

* * *

As life unfolds and the young choose their own paths, so Will set himself to his apprenticeship with all of his innate talents and the values instilled in him by his parents and family. He loved learning the intricacies of what he used to think were magical moments. He learned about heating and cooling. He learned how to hold the glowing iron. He very quickly learned that patterning was essential. There was foresight in all that came from the anvil's mighty surface.

His early years were busy, rising early in the morning, breakfasting and crossing the lane to the Smithy, loading the forge, setting the tools about the workplace, reviewing the list of the day's tasks. He had quickly learned that George knew very well what he expected of his new assistant. He was not one for conversation. He merely said, "This is how it is done." And then went about the daily work. Will learned from his observations to anticipate his next moves and learned to have the right tool in the right place at the right time. George had even told Will's father that he was a bright young man and a quick learner. He said that their work load could be increased due to the fact that Will's commitment to work made the work flow much better and more efficiently.

Will's father shared this with him around the table one evening and added, "It is so wonderful to see you make such rapid progress and have so much enjoyment in your work. I am sure you have found your calling." Will reflected on his father's pride in him and felt good about himself – and yes, he did love his work. He so loved the thud of the hammer on red-hot iron, leaving a trail of hammer blows, tracks in the iron he called them, marks that would stay for many years and cause those few wondering souls to imagine what was in the mind of the maker. He began thinking of "Markings," which were carved on stone, bone, tusks, trees, objects of all kinds. He thought that one day he too would leave some "markings" that would travel forward in time, long after the history he lived, and eventually replaced by new history.

Years passed and Will became the Smithy, or Wroughtist as he liked to call himself, when he spoke of his work to his lovely young wife. He and Sarah would spend Sunday mornings at the church attending Mass and later on they would return to mend what needed mending and clean up the graveyard. He had always had an affinity for "those who had gone before." Sarah knew of his devotion, as she had noticed his commitment when she passed by church on those afternoons when she was walking with the other girls from the village. And so it was that she made it a practice to stop and linger, arranging the flowers that were left as remembrances by those who wished their kin well. It hadn't taken long before Will had spoken to her and they began their quiet times sharing their feelings and their courting. He discussed how his family would read the Bible around the hearth and how his father and mother would discuss the various passages and ask their children about their thoughts about the meanings of the Gospels. He had said, "That is something that I want to do someday with my wife and with my children."

A year later, after Will had finished their new home, they were married and started their life together in a small cottage slightly uphill from Will's parents' home. He told Sarah he had decided that the best thing he could do was to prepare a place for his own family and create a space that could be added on for the coming children that he expected they would have.

And, as life would have it, those early commitments are some of our most foundational underpinnings. He and Sarah would share readings in the evenings as they sat before the hearth and spoke of those deepest dreams of young couples. They spoke of children, their aging parents, and fulfillments of deep joys.

One of those joys, Sarah knew, was that Will had in mind to create a work of art, an iron plaque that could hang in the vestibule of the church, something that could be there for the many generations, something that would cause a person to pause and reflect upon the message that he would leave for them. He spoke of different Biblical passages that he thought were especially inspiring and worthy of further reflection. He had often told Sarah that one of the most important things his father had taught him was the absolute need to reflect on one's own life and to always try and live a life that responded to the message of the Gospels. Upon occasion they also spoke of the news of the day, the "happenings" as Will would call them – as so many people were passing by the Smithy, coming to order this or that, and sharing what they had heard on their journeys. There were also those who came up the hill from the city. Their reputations were growing and their work was much in demand.

One afternoon, after returning from the graveyard, Will and his young wife were sitting in the late afternoon discussing the changing times and he mentioned that the Smithies of the city were forming a new Guild. They wanted to maintain an excellent record of production, and with the many people coming to the city from all parts of the country there were many charlatans and they did not want them to be giving their work a bad name. He mentioned that he would like to attend a meeting to see what advantages there might be in becoming a member. Sarah thought that would be a good idea. So many things were changing so rapidly. Will would say that "history is unfolding right before our eyes," as large numbers of people were moving about in the land and many new things were being brought in by ships from all over the known world. It was an exciting time.

Will had mentioned to Sarah his concerns that the guild might want to prohibit him from making anything he wanted, instead limiting his creativity, expecting him to make only the same things. They had been talking about specialization, with certain Smithies making only what they were permitted to do along with weights and measurements of all pieces to be set by some board of selectmen. He wasn't sure what being a member of a guild would entail, but he reasoned that it would be a good idea to stay informed.

The bustling activities of the port town of Bristol were rapidly turning the community into a city, and people were paying more and more attention to the many new developments. There were larger homes being built with iron railings surrounding courtyards, and large iron gates with locks and keys. Will was a very good locksmith himself and he knew that there would be much new business as the shipping trade expanded, including the Golden Triangle as some people were calling it – England, Africa, and the Americas.

There was also much discussion about the new trade for the slave ships and all of the accouterments necessary to outfit them, which were thought to be a large and growing part of the city's economy. There would be bolts, nuts, all manner of iron tools, small chains, collars, manacles, anchors, large chains, a plethora of objects – leaded whips, tongs, branding irons – the list seemed interminable. There was even a group of Smithies that wanted to approach the Company of Royal Adventurers Trading to Africa to gain a proprietary right to provide all of the necessary gear and what-not to the shipping industry.

After much reflection, Will finally decided that he would attend one of the Guild's meetings to get a better understanding of what the movement was all about. Afterward, he returned home and quietly told Sarah that there was, indeed, much to think about.

There were times when Will would walk alone in the hills to "set his thinking straight." Sarah knew that much of that time was spent praying. And often, Will would share that he was beginning to formulate a list of words that he thought would help those who could not read, and even those who could, to ponder the great needs of living a Christian life.

Will shared with Sarah how he felt about the limitations and the kinds of things, if he joined the Guild, that he would be required to manufacture. He said firmly that he would not make such things for the slave trade. He did not believe that human beings should be enslaved under any circumstances. Personal freedom had blossomed in the British Isles and there was a special appreciation for one's own sense of self-worth, and independence of character.

Parental pride was obvious when they would get together with his parents. Love was showered on each member of each generation, aging parents and their accomplishments, children and their current works, Sarah's homemaking prowess, and the grandchildren. Comments were made about their behavior, and about Will's grand projects. They spoke of the scrolls for the Stations of the Cross, the many faceted and grilled gates, as well as strong boxes for the parishes in the surrounding countryside and other things that Will was making as he continued to earn the respect and admiration of his patrons.

They were glad that he had retained his own independence and had not joined a Guild. He had chosen to acknowledge his own talents and to express them to the extent he could. He truly was an artisan, a freeman.

Will mentioned to Sarah that he had always wanted to create a crucifix as a solemn work of art – a work that would be his most personal expression of the Savior's ultimate gift to all humanity. Sarah knew that he prayed and thanked the Lord for his talents and the desire to create, all of which he attributed to God's infinite love for all his creations. Sarah also spent reflective hours in which she offered her own prayers of thanksgiving.

There were some phrases that Will had been formulating in his discussions with Sarah, his friends, his patrons, and the parish priest. They were simple concrete terms that could be understood by anyone who was willing to think about the most important things in living one's own dedicated life. As he mulled over his work, his life, and his meditations from his walks he began to write down these Stones, Rules, Words, or Phrases. He had no idea what to call them. So far his list consisted of *Play One*, from that Biblical admonition of saving one's own soul and the Shakespearian bent of self-coincidental words followed by actions, the archetypes of thinking, saying, and doing of human life. And *Stand Still in Silence*, that omnipresent need to be aware of one's participation in a greater picture, a greater effort, one needed that moment of reflection to set one's own intent in line with the Divine's efforts, as we understood them, and to complement them with our individual human effort.

There was also this dictum, which seemed of the utmost importance: *True/Not True – Mine/Not Mine*. While we could not know everything, we could know that we were, and that ultimately we are responsible for knowing enough to maintain a fidelity to our own participation in God's Great Plan.

Obviously there were the Ten Commandments that served as a personal and communal template for their commitments to follow the inspired scripture, and yet he felt that perhaps there was also a need to have some secular template that matched one's everyday ponderings, those conclusions that could be drawn from our everyday interactions with our own thoughts and with our relationships with others.

He had recently added *Own it Now!* to his list. He had to admit that when there was so much going on in his mind he had a personal difficulty holding on to each important thought long enough to categorize it for further mental and spiritual rumination – something that was dangerous, a task to get done in some time frame, an itinerant prayerful thank you for some blessing, or whatever. He had found in reading the Lives of the Saints that there was a common thread of behavior in their lives: they were efficiently focused on what really mattered in their relationship to God. He really felt that was all that mattered and yet it was not an easy thing to carry one's busy life-thoughts and be focused on the Divine Presence in all things. It was while reflecting upon how this was to be done that he hit upon the fifth Saying, Stone, whatever: *Act in Love.* It was as if St. Paul's admonition of "Faith, Hope, and Charity, and the greatest of these is Charity" had seeped into his mind and soul as some kind of omnipresent template.

As he worked in the rhythm of his craft, his mind's eye ever-watchful of his efforts, he saw his hammer landing on the target of his intentions – and yet there were times when his blows landed elsewhere and he became dissatisfied with his efforts. There were times when he was still young that his anger would flare and he would admonish himself, "I must learn to do better." He did, indeed, learn to do better in his practiced strokes and yet there were still times when he missed his mark. As he matured, his admonishments became softer and less accusatory. He began to realize that there was a certain omnipresent serendipity to the laws of physics or nature, as he was wont to call them, and in simple truths like wondering how many flowers in the meadow are perfect. He would always say, "None or all, and I choose to see them all as perfect in their own individual ways." He would also apply this to all of the different people that he met along the way. Sarah had told him many times that that was one of his most admirable attributes, that he always gave people the opportunity to be who they really were.

Will had even told Sarah that when he was working on a particular piece his mind would imagine other shapes and sizes that could have a more beautiful flare or more efficient aspect and he would file away the thought to give this or that idea more consideration when he had more time. He said that he was sure that this was all a part of his conversations with God, and at times it was God's way of reminding him that His ways were infinite, and that to experiment with different forms was a way of expressing thanks to the Creator. "Growing in faith" he called it. He had then added *Dedicate Yourself to Growth* to his list of Sayings, and with that came the realization that if that were the case, he had come full circle from his self-awareness and thankfulness in the acceptance of the ownership of self and to all those helpful other concepts and finally to the realization that it, whatever it was, was all part and parcel of The Holy, of all of creation.

He put that last realization down on his list: *A Holy Endeavor Is About To Begin!* In fact it had begun, was always beginning, and would continue to begin. In human life's confirmation of its awareness, it was also confirming all the other aspects of that life and therefore all of creation. When he had written the seventh admonition, in a startling realization, he came to the conclusion that everything was, indeed, one, really one to One. It was the trail of all of creation, and our acknowledgment of our awareness of our participation was a prayer of thanksgiving for our very life, both earthly and eternal.

He also thought, "If I were to put just ONE on my plaque no one would understand what I was saying." He thought of the words "no one" and burst into laughter. There was, indeed, never NO ONE, there was always SOMEONE, and that something was God with all of his creation. Life had become a holy endeavor, would always be a Holy endeavor, and would continue to be a Holy endeavor and to remember this as the fundamental truth would be the closest thing to a perfect earthly prayer that men could utter. Life was, indeed, a prayer, a secular prayer that at the human level mirrored the celestial paternoster, the Lord's Prayer.

As Will's life continued to unfold he came to know, in that maturing wisdom of age, that his children were an ever-present joy for him and his wife. The drafts that he would design prior to fabricating new pieces – the ones he would labor over late at night in the silence of the darkness and the flickering light of the lamp, long after the children were asleep – were a form of an acknowledging prayer.

Sarah was very proud of Will's talent and his work ethic. He was a good provider and they made substantial contributions to the church and she felt that her life with him was as close as she could get to thanking God for all of His blessings. She felt the true joy of being a person who was drinking from a very full glass of life itself. In her prayers, she was totally thankful for the gifts of her life.

Finally, Will decided that it was time to create his plaque and that he would stamp upon it letters that read THE RULES, as he had finally begun calling his few words/phrases. His delicate touch with the chisels in creating the letters would be, for him, one of his life's major accomplishments, one that he could leave for all others – those that would come after him and Sarah, and long after his children's children.

WILL'S PRAYER

I hold the iron hard,
yet bend it with Thy will.
For it is You,
who in all things feeds my hope,
and allows me to believe
that I will find You in all things.
For it is You
who manifests Yourself in all things,
in the omegas of Your roots,
the perfect circles of Your acorns' caps,
and the supple willow
of Your pliant saplings woven into baskets
holding treasures from the earth,
and Your sharp-tipped thorns
as arrows
that pierced the wild creatures
of our fare,
You, who set the fire in our hearts.
I see your presence in all things.
I thank You
for Your unending love for me,
my family, and all my fellowmen.
Amen! Alleluia!
Alleluia! Amen!

EPITAPH

Long ago, it was thought, a craftsman had spent some time and thought creating what they came to think of – when they discovered it in the ruins of a countryside church on the outskirts of Old Bristol – as a plaque, an iron scroll. It was of such fine work that the Archeological Museum of London called it one of the most amazing examples of metal artwork ever found in the British Isles.

It became known as The Wroughtist's Piece and it was prominently displayed in the entrance of the Great Museum where all those entering and leaving could reflect on "The Rules."

{Play One}

{Stand Still in Silence}

{True, Not True – Mine, Not Mine}

{Own it Now!}

{Act in Love}

{Dedicate Yourself to Growth}

{A Holy Endeavor is About to Begin}

THE RULES

Play One

Stand Still in Silence

True, Not True – Mine, Not Mine

Own it Now!

Act in Love

Dedicate Yourself to Growth

A Holy Endeavor Is About To Begin

"The Rules" are from *The Game of Life: A Player's Manual for Executives and Others*, available at pathtotheself.com or http://amzn.to/fOrqEi

www.ingramcontent.com/pod-product-compliance
Lightning Source LLC
Chambersburg PA
CBHW020011050426
42450CB00005B/425